Maths
made easy

Key Stage 1
ages 6-7
Advanced

Author
Sue Phillips

Consultant
Sean McArdle

LONDON • NEW YORK • MUNICH • MELBOURNE • DELHI

Numbers

Which numbers are the snakes hiding?

1	2	3	4	5		7	8	9	
11	12	13		15			18	19	
21	22	23	24		26	27	28		
31			35	36		38	39	40
41			45		47	48	49	50
	52	53	54	55		57	58	59	60
61		63	64	65				69	70
	73	74		76	77	78	79	80
81	82		84				88		
		93		95	96		98		

6

16 | 17

Read, write, and draw

Write the numbers and draw the pictures.

| 76 | seventy-six | |

| 59 | | |

| | forty-five | |

| 112 | one hundred and twelve | |

| | | |

| 107 | | |

| | one hundred and fifty | |

Counting

Count forwards or backwards in 10s.
Write the missing numbers.

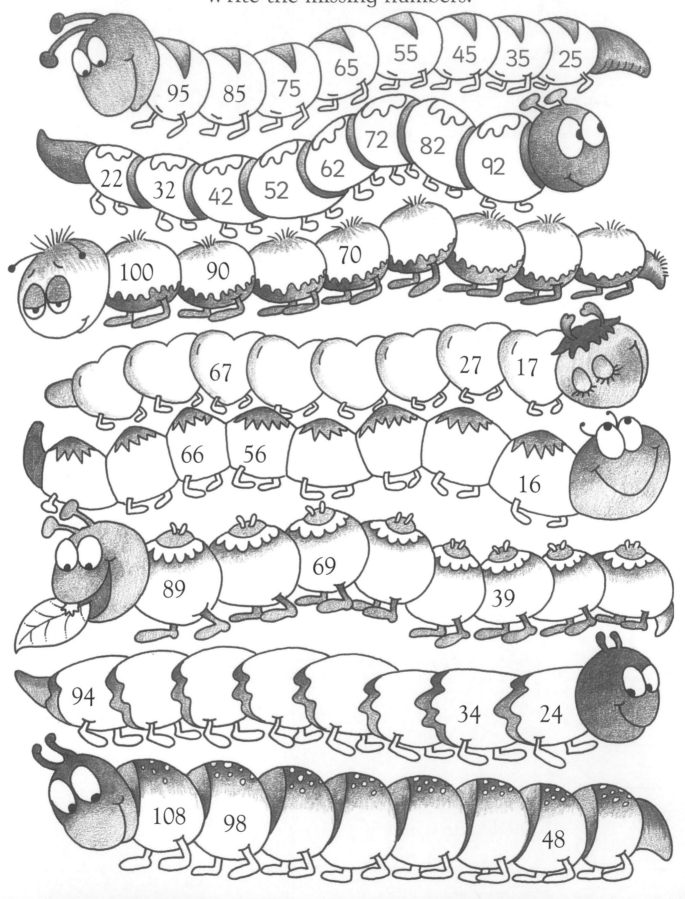

95 85 75 65 55 45 35 25

22 32 42 52 62 72 82 92

100 90 70

67 27 17

66 56 16

89 69 39

94 34 24

108 98 48

Odd or even?

Add or take away to find the answers to the sums.
Choose two colours. Colour the odd houses one colour
and the even houses another colour.

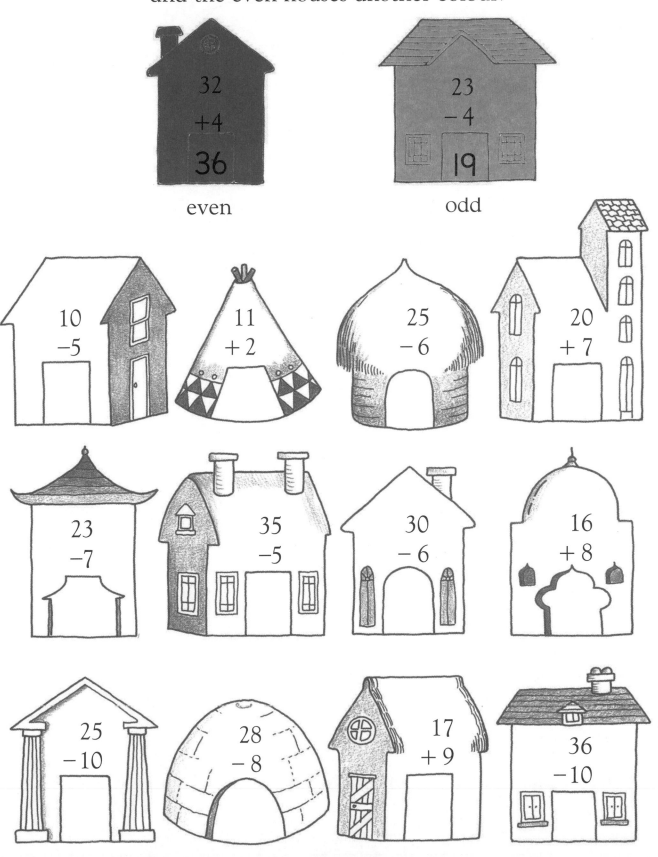

32
+4
36

even

23
−4
19

odd

10
−5

11
+2

25
−6

20
+7

23
−7

35
−5

30
−6

16
+8

25
−10

28
−8

17
+9

36
−10

Counting in 3s, 4s, and 5s

Draw, count, and write.

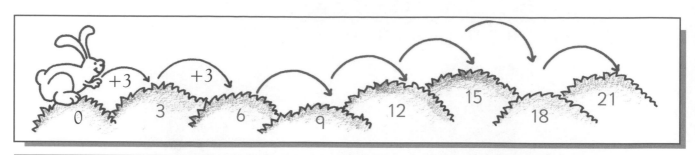

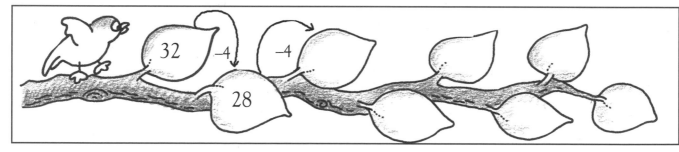

2s, 5s, and 10s

Use your 2x, 5x, and 10x tables to help you join the dots.

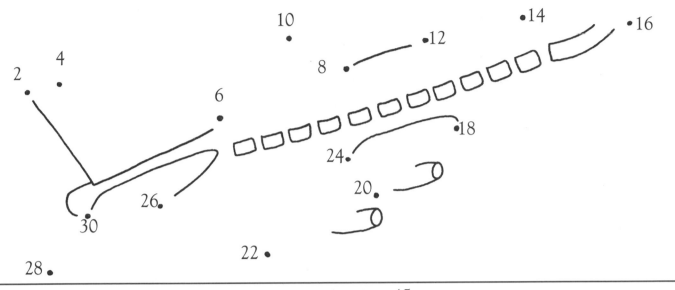

10
•14
•12
8
4
2
6
•16
•18
24•
26
20•
30
28•
22•

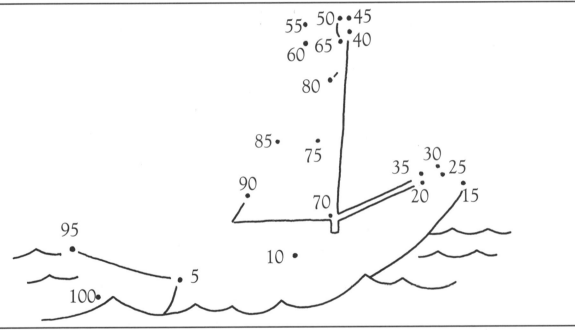

55• 50 •45
60 65 •40
80
85•
75
90
35 30 25
20 15
70
95
10•
5
100•

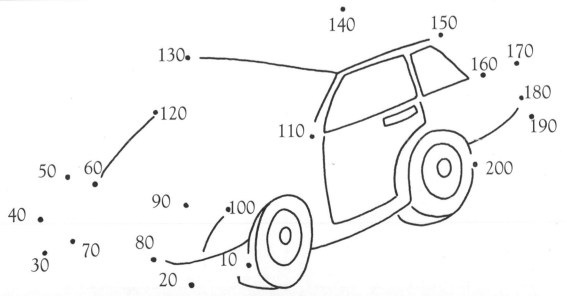

140 150
130•
160 170
•120
•180
110• 190
50 60
200
40
90 •100
80
30 70 10
20

Comparing

Complete the boxes.

2 less		2 more
51	53	55

	In-between		
96	97	98	99

	In-between	
20		24

3 less		3 more
	30	

2 less		2 more
	29	

	In-between	
18		22

	In-between	
131		134

10 less		10 more
	119	

5 less		5 more
	85	

	In-between	
40		45

	In-between	
99		102

5 less		5 more
	156	

Ordering

Find the totals.

£ 2.20

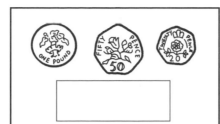

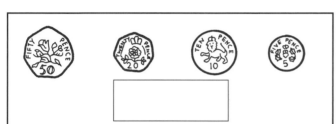

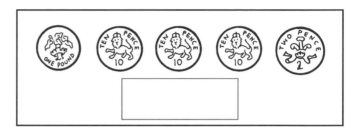

Write the totals in order, largest first.

| 1st £ 2.20 | 2nd | 3rd | 4th | 5th |

Find the totals.

92p

Write the totals in order, smallest first.

| 1st | 2nd 92p | 3rd | 4th | 5th |

Fractions

Colour one-third ($\frac{1}{3}$) and write how many.

$\frac{1}{3}$ of 9 is ☐ 3

$\frac{1}{3}$ of 12 is ☐

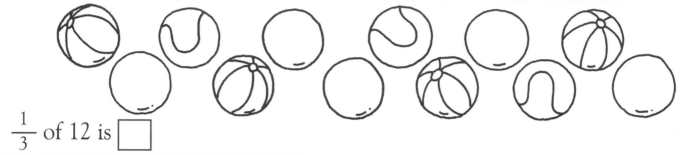

$\frac{1}{3}$ of 6 is ☐

$\frac{1}{3}$ of 3 is ☐

$\frac{1}{3}$ of 15 is ☐

$\frac{1}{3}$ of 18 is ☐

Matching fractions

Colour all the matching squares.

Use yellow for halves.
Use orange for thirds.
Use green for quarters.

$\frac{1}{2}$			
	one-third	one-half	
	$\frac{1}{4}$		one-quarter
$\frac{1}{3}$			

Label each part.

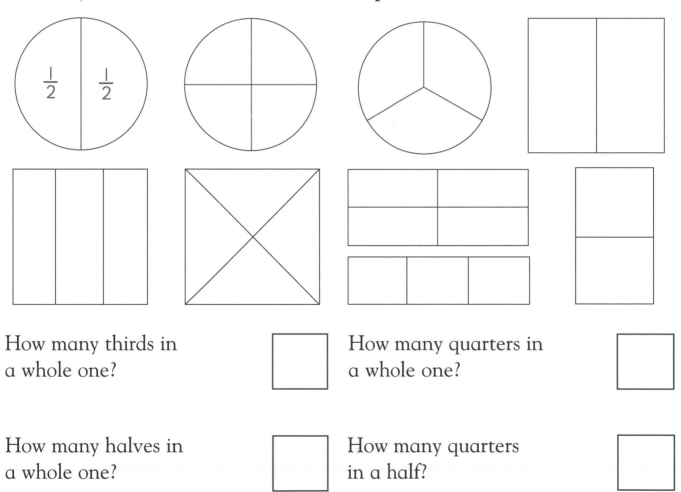

How many thirds in a whole one?

How many quarters in a whole one?

How many halves in a whole one?

How many quarters in a half?

Money

You have only 3 coins in each purse. Draw the
3 coins which make the exact amount needed.
You may use each coin more than once.

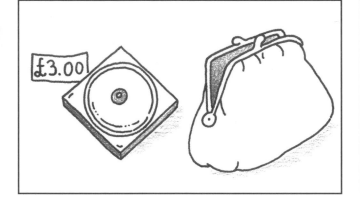

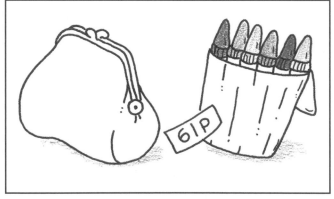

Number families

Use the 3 numbers to make 4 different sums.

6 + 7 = 13	7 + 6 = 13	13 − 7 = 6	13 − 6 = 7
16 + 4 = 20	+ =	− =	− =
6 5 11			
7 8 15			
8 12 20			
10 8 18			
8 9 17			
9 7 16			
14 6 20			
11 8 19			

Adding money

Add up the money. Write the totals in the right squares.

+	2p	5p	8p	6p
3p				9p
11p				
29p		34p		
32p				

+	2p	4p	6p	9p	3p
17p					
20p				29p	
33p	35p				
41p					

14

Using doubles

Use the doubles to answer these sums.

6 + 6 = 12	10 + 10 = 20
6 + 7 6 + 6 + 1 = 13	10 + 11 10 + 10 + 1 = 21
6 + 5 6 + 6 − 1 = 11	10 + 9 10 + 10 − 1 = 19

Use doubles to answer these sums.

4 + 4 = ☐   4 + 5 = ☐ + ☐ + 1 = ☐

4 + 3 = ☐ + ☐ − 1 = ☐

7 + 7 = ☐   7 + 8 = ☐ + ☐ + 1 = ☐

7 + 6 = ☐ + ☐ − 1 = ☐

8 + 8 = ☐   8 + 9 = ☐ + ☐ + 1 = ☐

8 + 7 = ☐ + ☐ − 1 = ☐

Double your doubles.

2	double it	4	double it	8	9	double it	☐	double it	☐
10	double it	☐	double it	☐	11	double it	☐	double it	☐
14	double it	☐	double it	☐	7	double it	☐	double it	☐

15

Adding up

Add up the numbers on the sails. Write the totals on the boats.

Add the numbers. Write the totals.

$3 + 4 + 12 =$ ☐ 19 $9 + 9 + 50 =$ ☐ $7 + 70 + 3 =$ ☐

$5 + 49 + 2 =$ ☐ $23 + 7 + 9 =$ ☐ $4 + 5 + 60 =$ ☐

$37 + 4 + 3 =$ ☐ $5 + 59 + 7 =$ ☐ $84 + 8 + 8 =$ ☐

$$\begin{array}{r} 39 \\ + 8 \\ + 7 \\ \hline \end{array}$$
$$\begin{array}{r} 18 \\ + 6 \\ + 5 \\ \hline \end{array}$$
$$\begin{array}{r} 57 \\ + 7 \\ + 4 \\ \hline \end{array}$$
$$\begin{array}{r} 66 \\ + 5 \\ + 0 \\ \hline \end{array}$$

Answer Section with Parents' Notes
Key Stage 1
Ages 6–7
Advanced

This 8-page section provides answers to all the activities in this book. This will enable you to mark your children's work or can be used by them if they prefer to do their own marking.

The notes for each page help explain the common pitfalls and problems and, where appropriate, give indications as to what practice is needed to ensure your children understand where they have gone wrong.

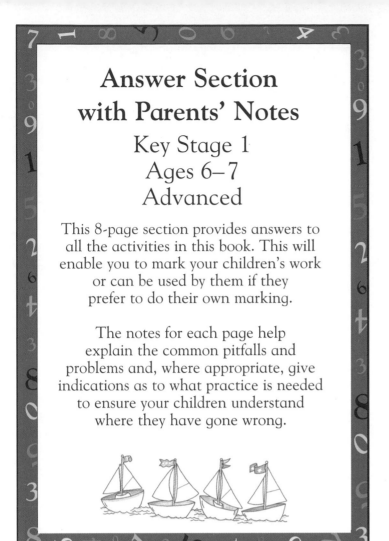

---

2 ⭐ ## Numbers

Which numbers are the snakes hiding?

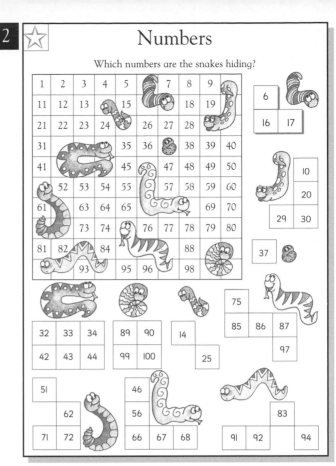

Ask the children how they can be sure that the numbers they have written in the boxes are the ones that have been hidden. Are they relying on only one strategy or are they looking at the columns as well as the rows?

---

3 ## Read, write, and draw ⭐

Write the numbers and draw the pictures.

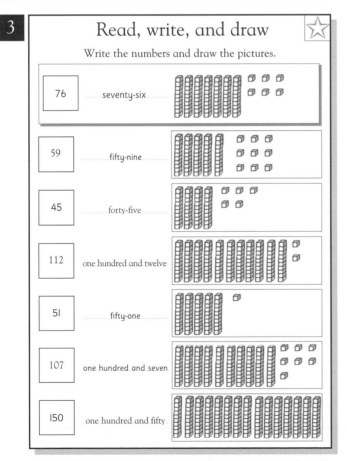

76	seventy-six
59	fifty-nine
45	forty-five
112	one hundred and twelve
51	fifty-one
107	one hundred and seven
150	one hundred and fifty

Do children remember the differing values of each digit? For example, in 170, the '1' is 100, the '7' is 70 and the '0' means no units. In 107, the '0' means no tens and the '7' is only 7 units.

---

4 ⭐ ## Counting

Count forwards or backwards in 10s.
Write the missing numbers.

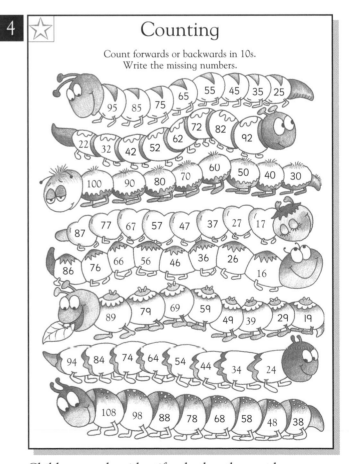

Children need to identify whether the numbers are getting smaller or larger, and whether that means they need to count on, or count backwards, by ten. Check that they realise the units digit always stays the same, while the tens digit goes up or down one each time.

Odd or even?

Add or take away to find the answers to the sums.
Choose two colours. Colour the odd houses one colour
and the even houses another colour.

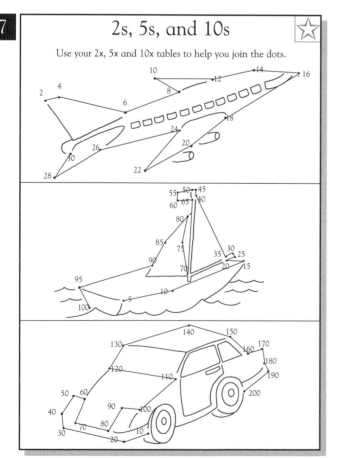

Houses shown with sums:

32 +4 = 36 even

23 −4 = 19 odd

10 −5 = 5

11 +2 = 13

25 −6 = 19

20 +7 = 27

23 −7 = 16

35 −5 = 30

30 −6 = 24

16 +8 = 24

25 −10 = 15

28 −8 = 20

17 +9 = 26

36 −10 = 26

Can children recite the even and odd sequences (2, 4, 6, 8, 10 and 1, 3, 5, 7, 9)? If they cannot spot a pattern in their answers, show them that starting with two even or two odd numbers always gives an even answer, regardless of whether they are adding or subtracting.

Counting in 3s, 4s, and 5s

Draw, count, and write.

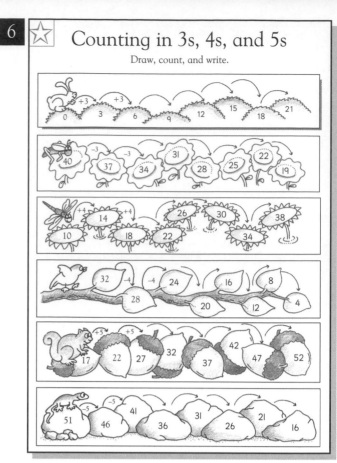

Row 1: 0, +3, 3, +3, 6, 9, 12, 15, 18, 21

Row 2: 40, −3, 37, −3, 34, 31, 28, 25, 22, 19

Row 3: 10, +4, 14, +4, 18, 22, 26, 30, 34, 38

Row 4: 32, −4, 28, −4, 24, 20, 16, 12, 8, 4

Row 5: 17, +5, 22, +5, 27, 32, 37, 42, 47, 52

Row 6: 51, −5, 46, −5, 41, 36, 31, 26, 21, 16

Remind children to check whether they should be adding or taking away. Subtracting or adding 5 creates a pattern, as the units in the answers go 7, 2, 7, 2 and 1, 6, 1, 6. Can they spot this and predict what the next numbers would be?

2s, 5s, and 10s

Use your 2x, 5x and 10x tables to help you join the dots.

Plane dots: 2, 4, 6, 8, 10, 12, 14, 16, 18, 20, 22, 24, 26, 28, 30

Boat dots: 45, 50, 55, 60, 65, 40, 80, 85, 90, 95, 100, 75, 70, 35, 30, 25, 20, 15, 10, 5

Car dots: 140, 150, 170, 160, 180, 190, 200, 130, 120, 110, 100, 90, 80, 70, 60, 50, 40, 30, 20, 10, 0

Check whether children can talk about the patterns in the number sequences. Can they recite the 2, 5, or 10 times tables, up to 10 times the number, before they start to join the dots?

Comparing

Complete the boxes.

2 less	In-between	2 more
51	53	55

1 less	In-between	1 more
96	97 98	99

1 less	In-between	1 more
20	21 22 23	24

3 less	In-between	3 more
27	30	33

2 less	In-between	2 more
27	29	31

1 less	In-between	1 more
18	19 20 21	22

1 less	In-between	1 more
131	132 133	134

10 less	In-between	10 more
109	119	129

5 less	In-between	5 more
80	85	90

1 less	In-between	1 more
40	41, 42, 43, 44	45

1 less	In-between	1 more
99	100 101	102

5 less	In-between	5 more
151	156	161

Check whether children can explain the meaning of more, less, and in-between. Can they give examples pertaining to smaller numbers (such as three more or less than 10)? The 'in-between' numbers have been varied so that answers do not follow the same format.

Ordering

Find the totals.

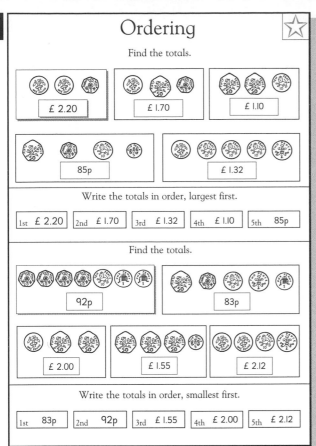

£ 2.20   £ 1.70   £ 1.10

85p   £ 1.32

Write the totals in order, largest first.

| 1st £ 2.20 | 2nd £ 1.70 | 3rd £ 1.32 | 4th £ 1.10 | 5th 85p |

Find the totals.

92p   83p

£ 2.00   £ 1.55   £ 2.12

Write the totals in order, smallest first.

| 1st 83p | 2nd 92p | 3rd £ 1.55 | 4th £ 2.00 | 5th £ 2.12 |

This page revises the operations of addition. No 'p' sign should be used with the '£' sign e.g. £1.50 not £1.50p. Help your child to talk about strategies for adding, e.g. does it help to add the larger or the smaller value coins first?

Fractions

Colour one-third $(\frac{1}{3})$ and write how many.

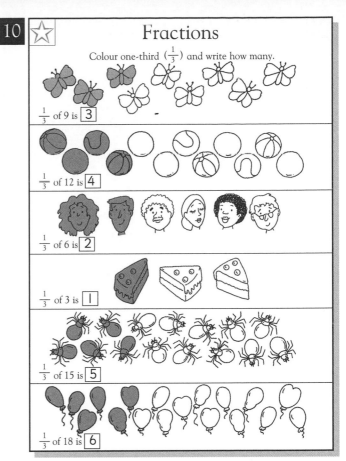

$\frac{1}{3}$ of 9 is 3

$\frac{1}{3}$ of 12 is 4

$\frac{1}{3}$ of 6 is 2

$\frac{1}{3}$ of 3 is 1

$\frac{1}{3}$ of 15 is 5

$\frac{1}{3}$ of 18 is 6

Help the children realise that the bottom number of the fraction indicates how many sets or groups they have to split the objects into.

Matching fractions

Colour the matching squares.

Use yellow for halves.
Use orange for thirds.
Use green for quarters.

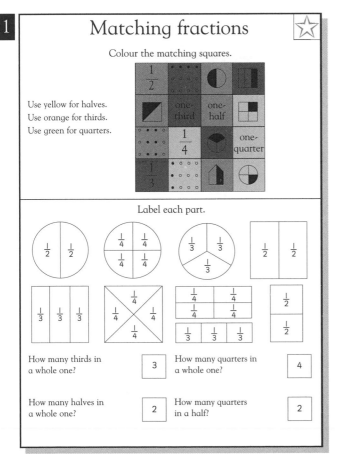

Label each part.

How many thirds in a whole one?   3

How many quarters in a whole one?   4

How many halves in a whole one?   2

How many quarters in a half?   2

If children answer the questions in the final section confidently, a suitable extension would be to ask such questions as, 'How many thirds are there in 3 whole ones?' 'If you had 12 quarters, how many whole ones would it make?'

Money

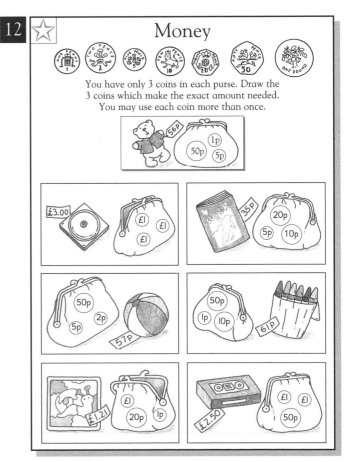

You have only 3 coins in each purse. Draw the 3 coins which make the exact amount needed. You may use each coin more than once.

56p — 50p 1p 5p

£3.00 — £1 £1 £1

35p — 20p 5p 10p

57p — 50p 5p 2p

61p — 50p 1p 10p

£1.21 — £1 20p 1p

£2.50 — £1 £1 50p

Limiting the number of coins makes children think more carefully about those they choose to use. It will be helpful to discuss this. They may need help to realise that it is sensible to look for the largest coin to be included first, rather than beginning with the units.

Number families

Use the 3 numbers to make 4 different sums.

6 + 7 = 13	7 + 6 = 13	13 – 7 = 6	13 – 6 = 7
16 + 4 = 20	4 + 16 = 20	20 – 4 = 16	20 – 16 = 4
6 + 5 = 11	5 + 6 = 11	11 – 5 = 6	11 – 6 = 5
7 + 8 = 15	8 + 7 = 15	15 – 7 = 8	15 – 8 = 7
8 + 12 = 20	12 + 8 = 20	20 – 8 = 12	20 – 12 = 8
10 + 8 = 18	8 + 10 = 18	18 – 10 = 8	18 – 8 = 10
8 + 9 = 17	9 + 8 = 17	17 – 9 = 8	17 – 8 = 9
9 + 7 = 16	7 + 9 = 16	16 – 9 = 7	16 – 7 = 9
14 + 6 = 20	6 + 14 = 20	20 – 14 = 6	20 – 6 = 14
11 + 8 = 19	8 + 11 = 19	19 – 11 = 8	19 – 8 = 11

This activity will help children see that if they know one combination of the numbers, then they really do know three other versions as well. If they know that 6+7=13 then, with a little practice, they will readily be able to give the answers to 7+6, 13–6 and 13–7.

Adding money

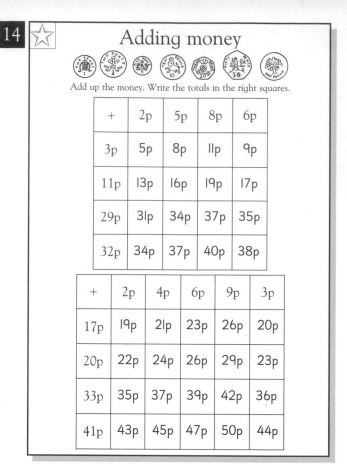

Add up the money. Write the totals in the right squares.

+	2p	5p	8p	6p
3p	5p	8p	11p	9p
11p	13p	16p	19p	17p
29p	31p	34p	37p	35p
32p	34p	37p	40p	38p

+	2p	4p	6p	9p	3p
17p	19p	21p	23p	26p	20p
20p	22p	24p	26p	29p	23p
33p	35p	37p	39p	42p	36p
41p	43p	45p	47p	50p	44p

Remind children that it is money they are adding here, therefore, they must write a 'p' for pence after each answer. Can they talk to you about any short-cuts they have noticed? For instance, when adding 9p, they could add 10p and then take 1p away.

Using doubles

Use the doubles to answer these sums.

6 + 6 = 12	10 + 10 = 20
6 + 7 6 + 6 + 1 = 13	10 + 11 10 + 10 + 1 = 21
6 + 5 6 + 6 – 1 = 11	10 + 9 10 + 10 – 1 = 19

Use doubles to answer these sums.

4 + 4 = 8　　4 +5 = 4 + 4 +1 = 9

4 +3 = 4 + 4 – 1 = 7

7 + 7 = 14　　7 + 8 = 7 + 7 +1 = 15

7 + 6 = 7 + 7 – 1 = 13

8 + 8 = 16　　8 + 9 = 8 + 8 +1 = 17

8 + 7 = 8 + 8 – 1 = 15

Double your doubles.

2	double it	4	double it	8	9	double it	18	double it	36
10	double it	20	double it	40	11	double it	22	double it	44
14	double it	28	double it	56	7	double it	14	double it	28

Recognising that a calculation involves two numbers that are almost the same is a useful skill. Doubling the number, and adding or subtracting the 'extra' bit, makes calculation far easier than counting with the whole numbers.

Adding up

Add up the numbers on the sails. Write the totals on the boats.

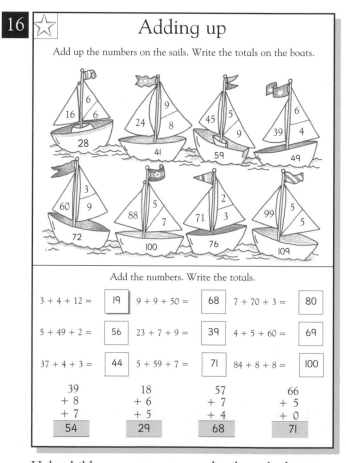

Add the numbers. Write the totals.

3 + 4 + 12 = 19　　9 + 9 + 50 = 68　　7 + 70 + 3 = 80

5 + 49 + 2 = 56　　23 + 7 + 9 = 39　　4 + 5 + 60 = 69

37 + 4 + 3 = 44　　5 + 59 + 7 = 71　　84 + 8 + 8 = 100

39	18	57	66
+ 8	+ 6	+ 7	+ 5
+ 7	+ 5	+ 4	+ 0
54	29	68	71

Help children spot ways to make the calculations easier, e.g. 24+9+8 is easier if they do 24+10+8 and then take one away. For the last boat they may need help to think in terms of 5+5 being added to 100, and the extra '1' being taken away from 110.

2x table

Draw the pictures. Write the number sentences.

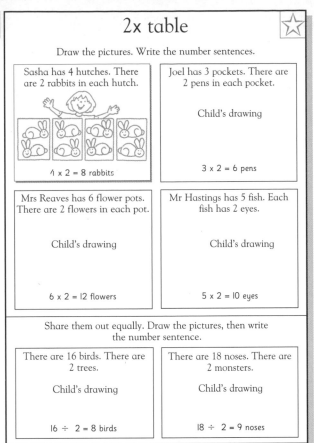

Sasha has 4 hutches. There are 2 rabbits in each hutch.

4 x 2 = 8 rabbits

Joel has 3 pockets. There are 2 pens in each pocket.

Child's drawing

3 x 2 = 6 pens

Mrs Reaves has 6 flower pots. There are 2 flowers in each pot.

Child's drawing

6 x 2 = 12 flowers

Mr Hastings has 5 fish. Each fish has 2 eyes.

Child's drawing

5 x 2 = 10 eyes

Share them out equally. Draw the pictures, then write the number sentence.

There are 16 birds. There are 2 trees.

Child's drawing

16 ÷ 2 = 8 birds

There are 18 noses. There are 2 monsters.

Child's drawing

18 ÷ 2 = 9 noses

As an extension, can your child make up their own simple stories using the 2x table? They could try writing and drawing.

10x table

Find the right label for each balloon. Only use the labels you really need.

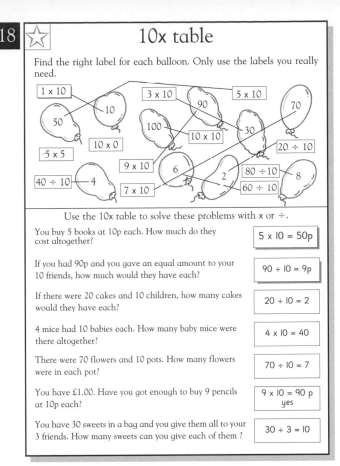

1 x 10   3 x 10   5 x 10   10   90   70   50   100   10 x 10   30   10 x 0   20 ÷ 10   5 x 5   9 x 10   6   80 ÷ 10   8   40 ÷ 10   4   7 x 10   2   60 ÷ 10

Use the 10x table to solve these problems with x or ÷.

You buy 5 books at 10p each. How much do they cost altogether?

5 x 10 = 50p

If you had 90p and you gave an equal amount to your 10 friends, how much would they have each?

90 ÷ 10 = 9p

If there were 20 cakes and 10 children, how many cakes would they have each?

20 ÷ 10 = 2

4 mice had 10 babies each. How many baby mice were there altogether?

4 x 10 = 40

There were 70 flowers and 10 pots. How many flowers were in each pot?

70 ÷ 10 = 7

You have £1.00. Have you got enough to buy 9 pencils at 10p each?

9 x 10 = 90 p yes

You have 30 sweets in a bag and you give them all to your 3 friends. How many sweets can you give each of them?

30 ÷ 3 = 10

Two labels not linked to any balloon have been put in to make children choose between answers. They should select answers carefully, deciding whether to multiply or divide. Trying out the language used earlier, 'shared between' for division and 'lots of' for multiplication, will help.

5x table

Find the right pot for each flower. Not all pots will have a flower.

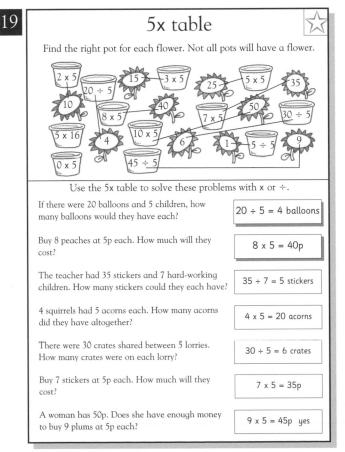

2 x 5   15   3 x 5   25   5 x 5   35   20 ÷ 5   10   40   8 x 5   50   7 x 5   30 ÷ 5   5 x 16   4   10 x 5   6   1   5 ÷ 5   9   0 x 5   45 ÷ 5

Use the 5x table to solve these problems with x or ÷.

If there were 20 balloons and 5 children, how many balloons would they have each?

20 ÷ 5 = 4 balloons

Buy 8 peaches at 5p each. How much will they cost?

8 x 5 = 40p

The teacher had 35 stickers and 7 hard-working children. How many stickers could they each have?

35 ÷ 7 = 5 stickers

4 squirrels had 5 acorns each. How many acorns did they have altogether?

4 x 5 = 20 acorns

There were 30 crates shared between 5 lorries. How many crates were on each lorry?

30 ÷ 5 = 6 crates

Buy 7 stickers at 5p each. How much will they cost?

7 x 5 = 35p

A woman has 50p. Does she have enough money to buy 9 plums at 5p each?

9 x 5 = 45p yes

The notes for page 18 are also relevant here. If children do not readily see that flower '1' links to 5÷5, it may help to say in words, 'If 5 (things) are shared out between 5 (people), how many would each get?' (1).

Calculators

Use a calculator and try out these keys.

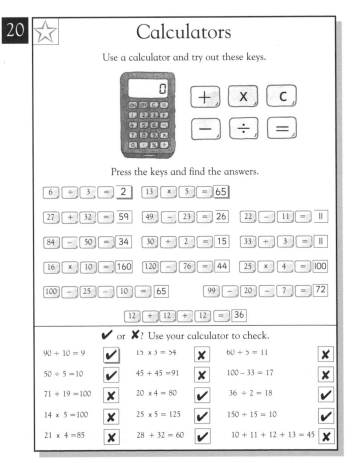

+   X   C   −   ÷   =

Press the keys and find the answers.

6 ÷ 3 = 2   13 x 5 = 65

27 + 32 = 59   49 − 23 = 26   22 − 11 = 11

84 − 50 = 34   30 ÷ 2 = 15   33 ÷ 3 = 11

16 x 10 = 160   120 − 76 = 44   25 x 4 = 100

100 − 25 − 10 = 65   99 − 20 − 7 = 72

12 + 12 + 12 = 36

✔ or ✘? Use your calculator to check.

90 ÷ 10 = 9 ✔	15 x 3 = 54 ✘	60 ÷ 5 = 11 ✘
50 ÷ 5 = 10 ✔	45 + 45 = 91 ✘	100 − 33 = 17 ✘
71 + 19 = 100 ✘	20 x 4 = 80 ✔	36 ÷ 2 = 18 ✔
14 x 5 = 100 ✘	25 x 5 = 125 ✔	150 ÷ 15 = 10 ✔
21 x 4 = 85 ✘	28 + 32 = 60 ✔	10 + 11 + 12 + 13 = 45 ✘

Encourage children to estimate an answer before they try the sum on the calculator. This will help them to query wrong answers due to pressing the wrong keys. Help them to develop the habit of doing each calculation twice for the same reason.

Real life problems

Look at the picture. Answer the questions.

What time is it ? __4:30__

Today is Friday. What day was it yesterday? __Thursday__

How many cakes can each person have? __two__

If half of the apples were eaten, how many would be left? __three__

If each person had 2 drinks, how many drinks would there be altogether? __eight__

How many more sandwiches are there than apples? __four__

If 13 sweets were eaten, how many would be left? __seven__

Each parcel contains 2 presents. How many presents are there altogether? __six__

What shape are the sandwiches? __triangle__

Is there an odd or an even number of chairs? __even__

Children will first have to decide what each question is asking them to do and then establish their own way of calculating the answer. For example, do they realise that the fifth question is asking for 4 x 2?

Real life problems

Complete the pictures, then write the sums.

There were 12 biscuits. James ate 3. How many were left?

$12 - 3 = 9$

Share 12 marbles equally between 3 people. How many marbles will each have?

$12 \div 3 = 4$

Susie has ten fish. She is given 11 more for her birthday. How many fish does she have altogether?

$10 + 11 = 21$

Joe had 5 boxes. He had 6 pencils in each box. How many pencils did he have altogether?

$6 \times 5 = 30$

If you share 20 carrots equally between 4 rabbits, how many carrots will each have?

$20 \div 4 = 5$

Mum had 16 cups, but she broke 9. How many cups has she got left?

$16 - 9 = 7$

When drawing, children should work out the operation they need, and which quantity is being shared or taken away. Do they know that in addition 4+5 and 5+4, or in multiplication 6 x 10 and 10 x 6, are the same, but that subtraction and division do not work this way?

Shopping

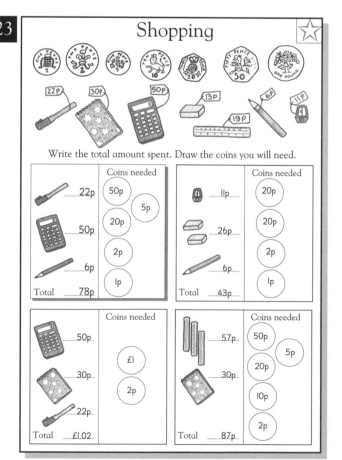

Write the total amount spent. Draw the coins you will need.

Coins needed

22p — 50p, 5p
50p — 20p, 2p
6p — 1p
Total __78p__

11p — 20p
26p — 20p, 2p
6p — 1p
Total __43p__

50p — £1
30p — 2p
22p
Total __£1.02__

57p — 50p, 5p
30p — 20p, 10p, 2p
Total __87p__

If children draw several lower value coins, to the right amount, praise them but explain the need to use fewer coins. They must write the unit (p or £) each time. There is no 'p' needed if a £ sign has already been used. Can they also record all their totals as decimals?

Clocks and watches

Write the times.

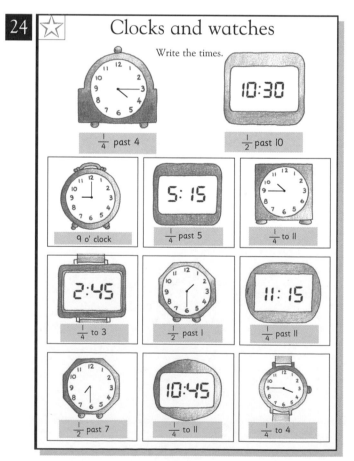

$\frac{1}{4}$ past 4

$\frac{1}{2}$ past 10

9 o' clock

$\frac{1}{4}$ past 5

$\frac{1}{4}$ to 11

$\frac{1}{4}$ to 3

$\frac{1}{2}$ past 1

$\frac{1}{4}$ past 11

$\frac{1}{2}$ past 7

$\frac{1}{4}$ to 11

$\frac{1}{4}$ to 4

Can children relate any of the times on the clocks to events in their own day? What do they do at $\frac{1}{4}$ to 4 or at 9 o'clock? Help them realise the need for the use of a.m. or p.m. in some cases, so that we can be certain if a time is in the morning, afternoon, or night.

More time

Look at the clocks and write the new times.

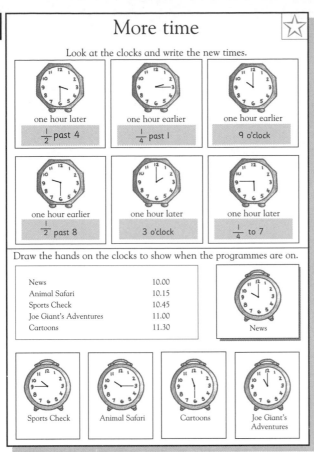

one hour later	one hour earlier	one hour earlier
½ past 4	¼ past 1	9 o'clock

one hour earlier	one hour later	one hour later
½ past 8	3 o'clock	¼ to 7

Draw the hands on the clocks to show when the programmes are on.

News	10.00
Animal Safari	10.15
Sports Check	10.45
Joe Giant's Adventures	11.00
Cartoons	11.30

News

Sports Check Animal Safari Cartoons Joe Giant's Adventures

It would be wise to check that the meanings of both 'earlier' and 'later' are fully understood. As an extension, can children draw the clocks, both analogue and digital, to show the times of their own favourite television programmes?

Tables and grids

Water animals

	Has 4 legs	Eats insects	Has a furry coat	Lays eggs
Frog	✓	✓	✗	✓
Newt	✓	✓	✗	✓
Otter	✓	✗	✓	✗

Use the grid to answer the questions.

What does the frog eat? **insects**   Who lays eggs? **frog, newt.**

Who has a furry coat? **otter**   Does the otter eat insects? **no**

Who has a furry coat and does not lay eggs? **otter**

School friends

	Age	Hobby	Pet	Favourite Colour
Dean	7	Computers	Rat	Black
Zoë	6	Reading	Rabbit	Purple
Taif	7	Judo	Cat	Orange
Maddie	8	Computers	Parrot	Green

Use the grid to answer the questions.

Whose favourite colour is black? **Dean's**   Who is the eldest? **Maddie**

Who has judo for a hobby? **Taif**   What kind of pet has Zoë got? **rabbit**

Who likes computers and has a parrot? **Maddie**   Who is seven and does not have a rat? **Taif**

If children find it difficult to focus on the box they can use two pencils or two fingers, and slide them along the row and down the column. Where they 'bump' is the right box. Techniques for reading simple grids will help them with complex ones later.

Venn diagrams

Things made of metal   Things made of plastic

How many things?

| Made of plastic | 6 | Made of metal | 7 |
| Made of metal and plastic | 3 | Not made of plastic | 4 |

Odd numbers   Numbers bigger than 20

3 15
1
7 19
21 25
24 26
30
22

How many numbers?

| Odd | 7 | Bigger than 20 | 6 |
| Odd and bigger than 20 | 2 | Not odd | 4 |

White things   Red things

How many things?

| Red | 5 | White | 6 |
| Red and white | 2 | Not red | 4 |

Children often forget to count the items in the intersection. Ask them to trace a finger around the set rings to reinforce the fact that they include the central section. Do they know, 'How many green things?' means that anything with green on it is included?

Carroll diagrams

	Can fly	Cannot fly
More than 2 legs	bee wasp	elephant giraffe mouse lizard
2 legs	duck sparrow hawk	penguin ostrich

How many creatures?

Cannot fly **6**   Have 2 legs and can fly **3**

Have more than 2 legs and cannot fly **4**

	Has 5 letters	Does not have 5 letters
Has a letter 'a'	Barry Tarik David Susan Geeta	Andrew Danielle Jade Rebecca Dean Olivia
Has no letter 'a'	Josie Lilly Cyril Steve Vicky	Sophie Lucy Jemille Justin

How many names?

With 5 letters **10**   With 5 letters but no 'a' **5**   With an 'a' **11**

	In the 5x table	Not in the 5x table
In the 2x table	10 30 20	14 12 6 2 4 8
Not in the 2x table	35 5 25 15	1 17 13 3 11 9 7

How many numbers?

In the 2x table **9**   In the 5x but not in the 2x table **4**

Not in the 2x or 5x tables **7**

Before answering any questions, ask your child to talk about each diagram and to give their own reasons why particular numbers or names are positioned where they are. They could also draw up their own questions to ask someone about the diagram.

Symmetry

Draw a line of symmetry on each picture.

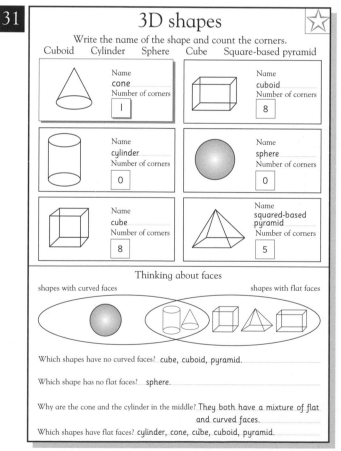

Draw lines of symmetry on these shapes.

Can children explain what a line of symmetry is? Can they relate this to their knowledge of halves having to be exactly the same? If they find this activity difficult they could draw shapes on paper and fold them in half to find the line of symmetry.

2D shapes

Write the name of the shape. Count the corners and sides.

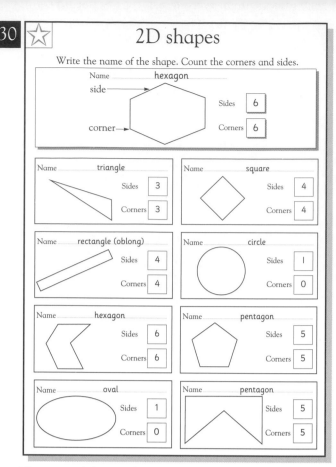

Name — hexagon

side →

corner →

Sides 6

Corners 6

Name triangle		Name square	
Sides	3	Sides	4
Corners	3	Corners	4

Name rectangle (oblong)		Name circle	
Sides	4	Sides	1
Corners	4	Corners	0

Name hexagon		Name pentagon	
Sides	6	Sides	5
Corners	6	Corners	5

Name oval		Name pentagon	
Sides	1	Sides	5
Corners	0	Corners	5

The second figure, though on its end, is still a square and not a diamond. Children may not recognise irregular shapes 5 and 8, but if they count the number of sides they should be able to name them according to that number. For example, any pentagon has 5 sides.

3D shapes

Write the name of the shape and count the corners.

Cuboid   Cylinder   Sphere   Cube   Square-based pyramid

Name cone
Number of corners
1

Name cuboid
Number of corners
8

Name cylinder
Number of corners
0

Name sphere
Number of corners
0

Name cube
Number of corners
8

Name squared-based pyramid
Number of corners
5

Thinking about faces

shapes with curved faces   shapes with flat faces

Which shapes have no curved faces? cube, cuboid, pyramid.

Which shape has no flat faces? sphere.

Why are the cone and the cylinder in the middle? They both have a mixture of flat and curved faces.

Which shapes have flat faces? cylinder, cone, cube, cuboid, pyramid.

If children find it difficult to count corners or to identify faces from the diagrams, let them find real examples of the shapes in the kitchen or their toy box. They could then begin to count the faces too. Can they see that a sphere only has one face?

Shapes and places

Look at the shapes and answer the questions.

circle
hexagon
oval
pentagon
rectangle
square
star
triangle

Which shape is ...

underneath the circle?	star
on the **left** of the triangle?	rectangle
above the hexagon?	square
below the pentagon?	oval
between the rectangle and the oval?	pentagon
diagonally above the empty space?	circle
by the side of the oval?	star
on top of the oval?	pentagon
between the triangle and the star?	circle
on the **right-hand end** of the top row?	square
in the **centre** of the grid?	circle
in the **top left-hand corner**?	rectangle

This page helps children to understand positional vocabulary. They may need help with the questions. It is not designed to test the spellings, so shapes are listed for reference. Try drawing an empty grid and giving instructions about where to write a number on it.

2x table

Draw the pictures. Write the number sentences.

Sasha has 4 hutches. There are 2 rabbits in each hutch.

4 x 2 = 8 rabbits

Joel has 3 pockets. There are 2 pens in each pocket.

Mrs Reaves has 6 flower pots. There are 2 flowers in each pot.

Mr Hastings has 5 fish. Each fish has 2 eyes.

Share them out equally. Draw the pictures, then write the number sentence.

There are 16 birds. There are 2 trees.

There are 18 noses. There are 2 monsters.

10x table

Find the right label for each balloon. Only use the labels you really need.

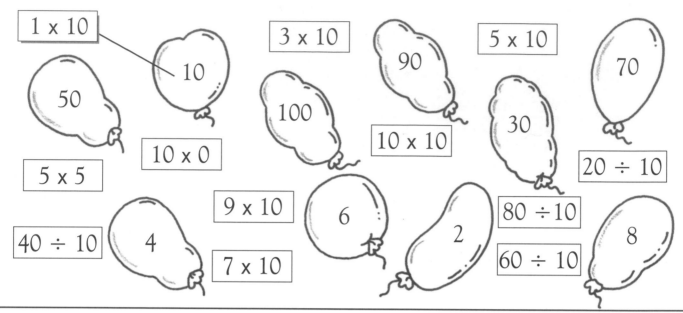

Use the 10x table to solve these problems with x or ÷.

You buy 5 books at 10p each. How much do they cost altogether?

$$5 \times 10 = 50p$$

If you had 90p and you gave an equal amount to your 10 friends, how much would they have each?

$$90 \div 10 = 9p$$

If there were 20 cakes and 10 children, how many cakes would they have each?

4 mice had 10 babies each. How many baby mice were there altogether?

There were 70 flowers and 10 pots. How many flowers were in each pot?

You have £1.00. Have you got enough to buy 9 pencils at 10p each?

You have 30 sweets in a bag and you give them all to your 3 friends. How many sweets can you give each of them ?

5x table

Find the right pot for each flower. Not all pots will have a flower.

Use the 5x table to solve these problems with x or ÷.

If there were 20 balloons and 5 children, how many balloons would they have each?

20 ÷ 5 = 4 balloons

Buy 8 peaches at 5p each. How much will they cost?

8 x 5 = 40p

The teacher had 35 stickers and 7 hard-working children. How many stickers could they each have?

4 squirrels had 5 acorns each. How many acorns did they have altogether?

There were 30 crates shared between 5 lorries. How many crates were on each lorry?

Buy 7 stickers at 5p each. How much will they cost?

A woman has 50p. Does she have enough money to buy 9 plums at 5p each?

Calculators

Use a calculator and try out these keys.

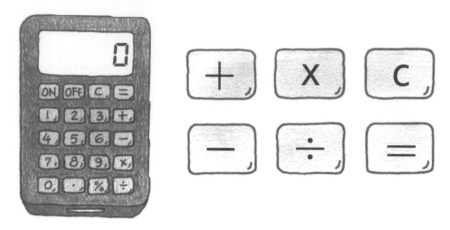

Press the keys and find the answers.

| 6 | ÷ | 3 | = | 2 | | 13 | x | 5 | = | 65 |

| 27 | + | 32 | = | ☐ | | 49 | − | 23 | = | ☐ | | 22 | − | 11 | = | ☐ |

| 84 | − | 50 | = | ☐ | | 30 | ÷ | 2 | = | ☐ | | 33 | ÷ | 3 | = | ☐ |

| 16 | x | 10 | = | ☐ | | 120 | − | 76 | = | ☐ | | 25 | x | 4 | = | ☐ |

| 100 | − | 25 | − | 10 | = | ☐ | | 99 | − | 20 | − | 7 | = | ☐ |

| 12 | + | 12 | + | 12 | = | ☐ |

✔ or ✘? Use your calculator to check.

90 ÷ 10 = 9	✔	15 x 3 = 54	✘	60 ÷ 5 = 11	☐
50 ÷ 5 = 10	☐	45 + 45 = 91	☐	100 − 33 = 17	☐
71 + 19 = 100	☐	20 x 4 = 80	☐	36 ÷ 2 = 18	☐
14 x 5 = 100	☐	25 x 5 = 125	☐	150 ÷ 15 = 10	☐
21 x 4 = 85	☐	28 + 32 = 60	☐	10 + 11 + 12 + 13 = 45	☐

Real life problems

Look at the picture. Answer the questions.

What time is it ? ....

Today is Friday. What day was it yesterday? ....

How many cakes can each person have? ....

If half of the apples were eaten, how many would be left? ....

If each person had 2 drinks, how many drinks would there be altogether? ....

How many more sandwiches are there than apples? ....

If 13 sweets were eaten, how many would be left? ....

Each parcel contains 2 presents. How many presents are there altogether? ....

What shape are the sandwiches? ....

Is there an odd or an even number of chairs? ....

Real life problems

Complete the pictures, then write the sums.

There were 12 biscuits. James ate 3. How many were left?

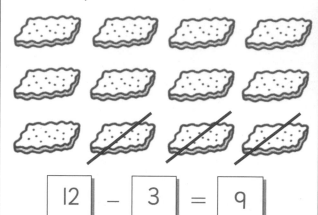

$$\boxed{12} - \boxed{3} = \boxed{9}$$

Share 12 marbles equally between 3 people. How many marbles will each have?

$$\boxed{} \div \boxed{} = \boxed{}$$

Susie has ten fish. She is given 11 more for her birthday. How many fish does she have altogether?

$$\boxed{} \quad \boxed{} = \boxed{}$$

Joe had 5 boxes. He had 6 pencils in each box. How many pencils did he have altogether?

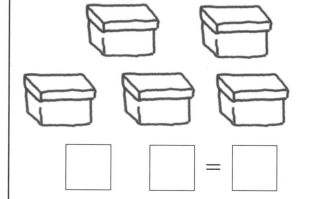

$$\boxed{} \quad \boxed{} = \boxed{}$$

If you share 20 carrots equally between 4 rabbits, how many carrots will each have?

$$\boxed{} \quad \boxed{} = \boxed{}$$

Mum had 16 cups, but she broke 9. How many cups has she got left?

$$\boxed{} \quad \boxed{} = \boxed{}$$

Shopping

Write the total amount spent. Draw the coins you will need.

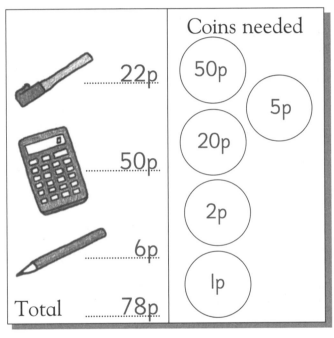

Coins needed

22p

50p

6p

50p   5p   20p   2p   1p

Total 78p

Coins needed

....

....

....

Total ....

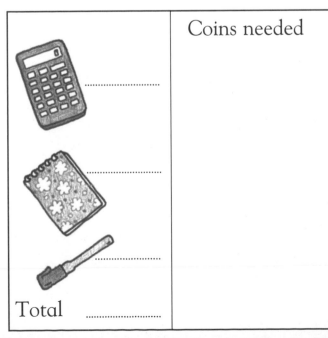

Coins needed

....

....

....

Total ....

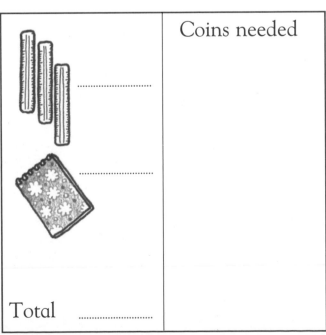

Coins needed

....

....

Total ....

23

Clocks and watches

Write the times.

$\frac{1}{4}$ past 4

$\frac{1}{2}$ past 10

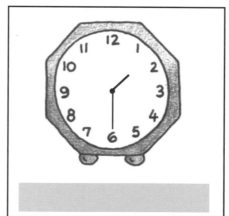

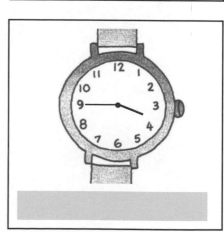

More time

Look at the clocks and write the new times.

one hour later

$\frac{1}{2}$ past 4

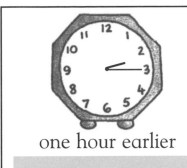

one hour earlier

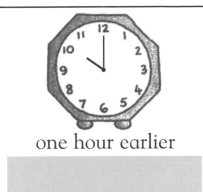

one hour earlier

one hour earlier

one hour later

one hour later

Draw the hands on the clocks to show when the programmes are on.

News	10.00
Animal Safari	10.15
Sports Check	10.45
Joe Giant's Adventures	11.00
Cartoons	11.30

News

Sports Check

Animal Safari

Cartoons

Joe Giant's
Adventures

Tables and grids

Water animals

	Has 4 legs	Eats insects	Has a furry coat	Lays eggs
Frog	✓	✓	✗	✓
Newt	✓	✓	✗	✓
Otter	✓	✗	✓	✗

Use the grid to answer the questions.

What does the frog eat? <u>insects</u>

Who lays eggs? _____

Who has a furry coat? _____

Does the otter eat insects? _____

Who has a furry coat and does not lay eggs? _____

School friends

	Age	Hobby	Pet	Favourite Colour
Dean	7	Computers	Rat	Black
Zoë	6	Reading	Rabbit	Purple
Taif	7	Judo	Cat	Orange
Maddie	8	Computers	Parrot	Green

Use the grid to answer the questions.

Whose favourite colour is black? <u>Dean's</u>

Who is the eldest? _____

Who has judo for a hobby? _____

What kind of pet has Zoë got? _____

Who likes computers and has a parrot? _____

Who is seven and does not have a rat? _____

Venn diagrams

Things made of metal   Things made of plastic

How many things?

Made of plastic   6   Made of metal   7

Made of metal and plastic   3   Not made of plastic   4

Odd numbers   Numbers bigger than 20

3   15
1
7   19
21   25
24   26
22
30

How many numbers?

Odd   ☐   Bigger than 20   ☐

Odd and bigger than 20   ☐   Not odd   ☐

White things   Red things

How many things?

Red   ☐   White   ☐

Red and white   ☐   Not red   ☐

27

Carroll diagrams

	Can fly	Cannot fly
More than 2 legs	bee wasp	elephant giraffe mouse lizard
2 legs	duck sparrow hawk	penguin ostrich

How many creatures?

Cannot fly   **6**

Have 2 legs and can fly   **3**

Have more than 2 legs and cannot fly   **4**

	Has 5 letters	Does not have 5 letters
Has a letter 'a'	Barry Tarik David Susan Geeta	Andrew Danielle Jade Rebecca Dean Olivia
Has no letter 'a'	Josie Lilly Cyril Steve Vicky	Sophie Lucy Jemille Justin

How many names?

With 5 letters

With 5 letters but no 'a'

With an 'a'

	In the 5x table	Not in the 5x table
In the 2x table	10 30 20	14 12 6 2 4 8
Not in the 2x table	35 5 25 15	1 17 13 3 11 9 7

How many numbers?

In the 2x table

In the 5x but not in the 2x table

Not in the 2x or 5x tables

28

Symmetry

Draw a line of symmetry on each picture.

Draw lines of symmetry on these shapes.

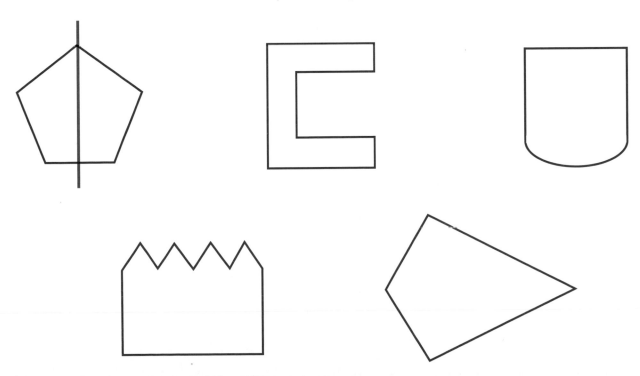

2D shapes

Write the name of the shape. Count the corners and sides.

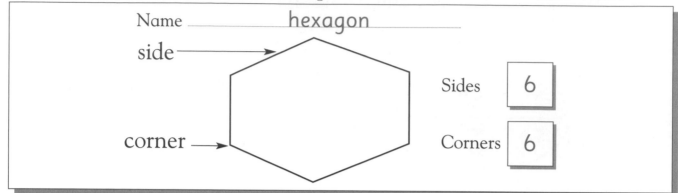

Name _____ hexagon

side →

corner →

Sides 6

Corners 6

Name _____

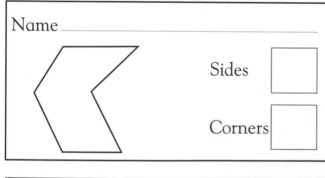

Sides

Corners

Name _____

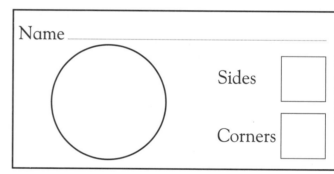

Sides

Corners

Name _____

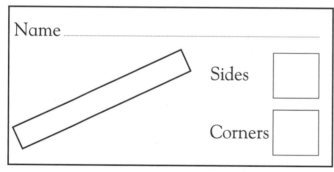

Sides

Corners

Name _____

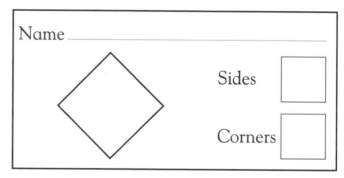

Sides

Corners

Name _____

Sides

Corners

Name _____

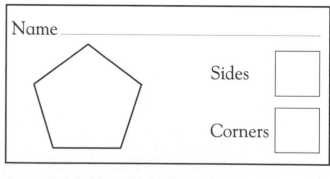

Sides

Corners

Name _____

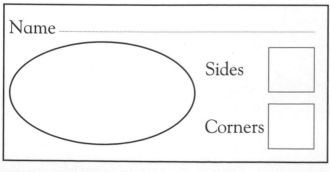

Sides

Corners

Name _____

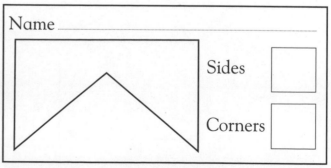

Sides

Corners

3D shapes

Write the name of the shape and count the corners.

Cuboid   Cylinder   Sphere   Cube   Square-based pyramid

Name
cone

Number of corners

1

Name

Number of corners

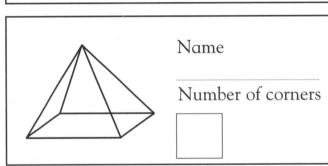

Name

Number of corners

Name

Number of corners

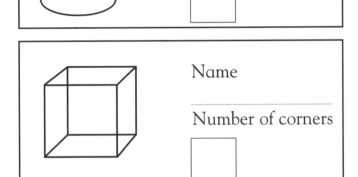

Name

Number of corners

Name

Number of corners

Thinking about faces

shapes with curved faces   shapes with flat faces

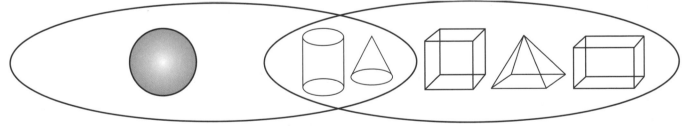

Which shapes have no curved faces?_____

Which shape has no flat faces?_____

Why are the cone and the cylinder in the middle?_____

_____

Which shapes have flat faces?_____

Shapes and places

Look at the shapes and answer the questions.

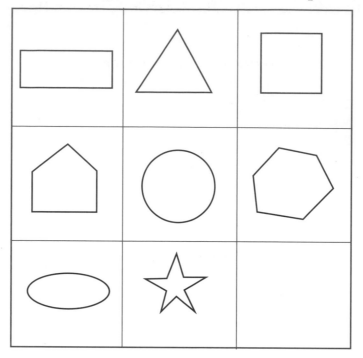

circle

hexagon

oval

pentagon

rectangle

square

star

triangle

Which shape is ...

underneath the circle? ....

on the **left** of the triangle? ....

above the hexagon? ....

below the pentagon? ....

between the rectangle and the oval? ....

diagonally above the empty space? ....

by the side of the oval? ....

on top of the oval? ....

between the triangle and the star? ....

on the **right-hand end** of the top row? ....

in the **centre** of the grid? ....

in the **top left-hand corner**? ....